· REDISCOVERING RAILWAYS ·

BERKSHIRE

$\begin{smallmatrix}(12)\\(46)\end{smallmatrix}$ SOUTHERN RAILWAY Stock 34GA

TO ....

G. W. Rly.
Via READING

Gt. Western Ry.	Gt. Western Ry
CHEAP RETURN	CHEAP TICKET
For day of issue by	For day of issue by
trains as advertised	trains as advertised
Basingstoke to	READING (4) to
READING (4)	BASINGSTOKE
THIRD CLASS	THIRD CLASS
SEE CONDITIONS ON BACK J.D.	

557   557

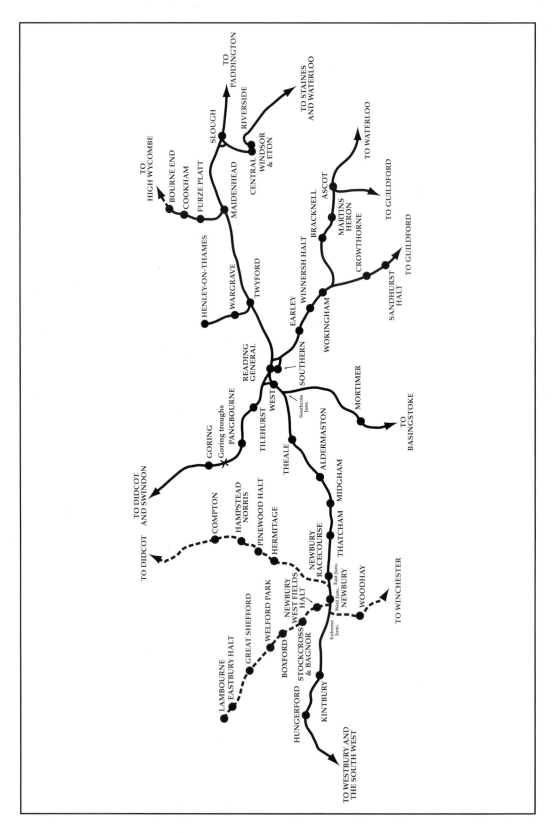

Map of the railways of Berkshire, showing the principal locations and others illustrated in the book.

· REDISCOVERING RAILWAYS ·

BERKSHIRE

A pictorial record of the county's railways past and present

Terry Gough

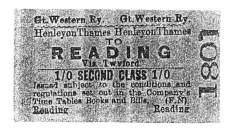

·RAILWAY HERITAGE·
from
The NOSTALGIA Collection

First published in 2002

British Library Cataloguing in Publication Data

A catalogue record for this book is available from the British Library.

ISBN 1 85895 174 7

Past & Present Publishing Ltd
The Trundle
Ringstead Road
Great Addington
Kettering
Northants NN14 4BW

Tel/Fax: 01536 330588
email: sales@nostalgiacollection.com
Website: www.nostalgiacollection.com

Some of the material in this book first appeared in *British Railways Past and Present, No 21 Berkshire and Hampshire*, by the same author and published by Past & Present Publishing Ltd in 1994.

All tickets and other items of ephemera are from the author's collection.

Printed and bound in Great Britain

A Past & Present book
from
The NOSTALGIA Collection

CONTENTS

Left and below **NEWBURY: An express approaches Newbury from the west in the 1970s. On the right is the Lambourn branch and well beyond the overbridge in the background is the junction with the line from Winchester. Today's express, passing the same point but with no sign of the Lambourn branch, is the 08.05 Penzance to Paddington on 17 March 1999. The leading power car is Class 43 No 43005.** *D. E. Canning/TG*

READING GENERAL: 'King' Class No 6018 *King Henry VI* approaches Reading on a down express in 1958, before any serious threat of diesels. Plenty has changed at Reading since then, with the rebuilding of the station including new platforms for trains to Waterloo and the Guildford line, seen on the right-hand side. On 20 June 2001 a Class 47 in First Great Western livery works the 16.33 Paddington to Penzance train. *Great Western Trust, courtesy Laurence Waters/TG*

INTRODUCTION

The Great Western Railway (GWR) main line from Paddington cut through Berkshire, with the county town of Reading the first stop for many of the long-distance trains. Reading was also reached by the London & South Western Railway (LSWR) from Waterloo, and the South Eastern Railway (SER) from Kent, both of which had several stations in Berkshire. All these lines are still open. Reading itself has changed almost out of recognition with the closure of the former Southern Region station, the rebuilding of the Western Region station and the surrounding land redevelopment. The SR and GWR engine sheds have gone, and the latter site is occupied by a diesel multiple unit (DMU) depot. Reading is also the junction for the GWR lines to Basingstoke and Newbury (for the West of England), while the Bristol and South Wales line leaves the county near Goring. The north-south route of the Didcot, Newbury & Southampton Railway is completely closed, although there is evidence of its former route in many places. The GWR built branch lines to Henley-on-Thames, High Wycombe, Lambourn and Windsor, and the latter was also reached from Waterloo by the LSWR. Only the Lambourn branch has been closed, although the High Wycombe line has been truncated beyond Bourne End.

On almost all of these lines steam was seen until at least the 1950s. Expresses on the GWR were worked by 'Kings', 'Castles' and 'Halls', and latterly by 'Britannias'. In contrast, the SR trains were worked by an antiquated collection of pre-grouping locomotives, with a handful of BR Standard locomotives towards the end of steam. Exceptions were the inter-Regional trains with Bulleid 'Pacifics', the SR trains from Waterloo, which were electric, and the diesel railcars used on the WR Windsor and Lambourn branches. Both these forms of motive power had been introduced in the

1930s on these lines. The WR introduced the 'Warship' Class diesel-hydraulic locomotives in 1958 and the 'Western' Class in 1961, but by the end of 1970 most had been withdrawn. On secondary routes and branch lines DMUs took over from steam. In 1976 the WR moved away from the use of locomotives on express trains, with the introduction of high-speed InterCity 125 trains. which are still the mainstay of almost all long-distance trains. The use of locomotives on all services has almost been eliminated with the recent introduction of second-generation DMUs (the 'Thames Turbos'). These units have also replaced what are now termed 'Heritage' DMUs from both the WR branch lines and the SR line from Guildford. There are still a few remaining locomotive-hauled passenger trains. These are almost all Virgin Cross Country services, with a few re-introduced on First Great Western trains in the summer of 2001. All are expected to be eliminated during 2002.

There is heavy freight traffic on the main line, and the Berks & Hants line in particular has a frequent flow of stone trains. Freightliner trains operating between the Midlands and Southampton pass through the county, and there are many infrastructure movements. All this makes for an interesting visit, particularly to the Reading area. This book is a record of the changes that have taken place since the 1950s in both the trains and the stations they serve.

I have taken the traditional county boundary and have excluded those stations on the main line that were formerly in Buckinghamshire; these are covered in *British Railways Past and Present No 13*.

Terry Gough
Sherborne, Dorset

ACKNOWLEDGEMENTS

It has been an enjoyable experience to revisit the places shown in the following pages, in some cases after a gap of about 40 years. There were, however, a number of locations for which I had no material, mostly on ex-GWR lines, as a lack of resources when I was younger forced me to restrict my visits to SR territory. I am therefore pleased to acknowledge the support of the several colleagues named in the captions who have kindly provided material from their collections to fill the gaps. Much of my own 1960s material was taken on the railway side of the fence and I gratefully acknowledge the willingness of the railway authorities to allow access. The disappearance of goods yards has allowed closer public viewing of the railway and has meant that in most cases it has been easy to align 'past' and 'present' photographs, sometimes with the assistance of the telephoto lens. Some former stations are now privately owned, and I thank those owners who allowed me on to their properties. I thank Colin Pattle and Dick Ware for information on present practice. Finally I thank my wife Cynthia for encouragement to complete this revised edition on time.

BIBLIOGRAPHY

British Railways Past and Present No 13, North West, West and South West London, Brian Morrison & Ken Brunt (Past & Present, 1992)

British Railways Past and Present No 15, Oxfordshire, Laurence Waters & Tony Doyle (Past & Present, 1992)

The Didcot, Newbury & Southampton Railway, T. B. Sands (Oakwood Press)

Lambourn Valley Railway, M. R. C. Price (Oakwood Press)

Rail Centres, Reading, Laurence Waters (Ian Allan)

Rediscovering Railways: Hampshire, The north of the county, Terry Gough (Past & Present, 2001)

A Regional History of the Railways of Great Britain, Volume 2, H. P. White, and *Volume 13*, R. Christiansen (David & Charles)

Southern Railway Reflections: Surrey and Berkshire, Terry Gough (Past & Present, 1999)

LINES FROM PADDINGTON

Windsor branch

WINDSOR & ETON CENTRAL (1): Changes in county boundaries have brought some former Buckinghamshire stations into Berkshire, including Slough on the GWR main line. From here there is a short branch to Windsor, where

the terminus was a large and imposing building and had a frequent service. On 18 July 1955 Class 6100 No 6143 works the branch train.

The line is still open, but there is now only one shortened platform in use, as seen in April 1993. A hairdresser still occupies the same position and has acquired a new entrance to his salon. Boutiques and other tourist attractions are also to be found on the forecourt. In the background is the 'Royalty and Empire' exhibition centre, and beyond that is a large car park under the protection of an all-over roof, once part of the railway. *Alan Jackson/TG*

WINDSOR & ETON CENTRAL (2): The branch was regularly worked by GWR diesel railcars until the advent of the first BR-built DMUs. The 1999 photograph of the same location gives the impression that there is no longer a railway here. In fact, all that has happened is a further shortening of the platform (see page 9). The station still has a very frequent service to and from Slough. *Laurence Waters/TG*

WINDSOR & ETON CENTRAL (3): This undated photograph shows GWR railcar No W27W entering the station following the short run from Slough. In March 1999 the train consists of Class 165 No 165003, entering the station on the only remaining line. The site of the other lines into the station and the carriage sidings is now occupied by the cars. *Bob Barnard, courtesy Hugh Davies/TG*

WINDSOR & ETON CENTRAL (4): Two single-car DMUs are seen leaving Windsor on 9 March 1968. First-generation BR DMUs were still in use in 1993, as shown by the second photograph of No 263 on 4 April. This unit consists of one coach of Class 104 and the other of Class 121. *Edwin Wilmshurst/TG*

Shortening of the only remaining platform and removal of all other lines precludes the use of long trains such as this special seen leaving Windsor on 6 June 1953. The engine is ex-Great Central Railway 'Director' Class (D11) No 62666 *Zeebrugge* and the train is the 'Northern Rubber Special'. *Neil Sprinks*

LINES FROM PADDINGTON

Maidenhead to Reading and branches

MAIDENHEAD (1) has always been in Berkshire, and a down freight approaches on 26 March 1959 hauled by Class 5700 No 3697 of Slough shed. The up and down fast lines are on the far right.

Freight now is mainly in the form of oil, stone and Freightliners. I was waiting for one of the afternoon empty stone trains on 24 March 1994 when a single-car DMU came hurtling along the main line towards Reading. It was identified as Class 121 No L128 (977860), which is used as a route-learning and Sandite vehicle. *Andrew C. Ingram/TG*

MAIDENHEAD (2): There are four tracks through Maidenhead, the pair nearest the camera being the main lines, the up line on 3 April 1956 being occupied by a double-headed express from South Wales. The engines are both 'Castle' Class, Nos 7006 *Lydford Castle* and 7035 *Ogmore Castle*.

The down main platform and up main face of the island platform had been unused for several years, but in 1999 they were refurbished and some peak-hour trains on the main lines now call at Maidenhead. The other two lines are used for stopping trains and most of the freight movements. On 24 May 2001 Class 47 No 47722 *The Queen Mother* is on the up main line with the 07.08 Manchester Piccadilly to Brighton train, which runs via Kensington Olympia and East Croydon. *Great Western Trust, courtesy Laurence Waters/TG*

FURZE PLATT: From Maidenhead there was a line to High Wycombe, which was closed beyond Bourne End in 1970. The first and only station on this line in Berkshire was Cookham, but a halt was built at Furze Platt in 1937, seen here looking towards High Wycombe on 28 October 1966.

Furze Platt is still open, and a train is seen approaching on the morning of 20 April 1993 consisting of Class 101 DMU No L200. *Alan Jackson/TG*

COOKHAM: This early photograph of Cookham is looking towards Bourne End. With singling of the line the footbridge and down platform became redundant, and although the footbridge has been removed, the facing of the old platform now separates the car park from the railway. The iron railings have been repositioned along the facing, while the station buildings on the down side are in use as offices and a warehouse. On the operating side the traditional facilities of a waiting room and toilets are still available. On 23 March 1999 Class 165 No 165004 enters the station on an early afternoon train to Maidenhead. *Lens of Sutton/TG*

Opposite TWYFORD (1) is the next main-line station, and the several road overbridges nearby give excellent views of the railway. In the 'past' view down trains on both the fast and local lines are seen just east of the station in the late 1950s. The train on the right is hauled by 'Hall' Class No 4948 *Northwick Hall*.

In the summer of 2001 First Great Western replaced its HST125 units with Class 47 locomotive-hauled trains on some of its West of England services. This is the 15.42 Paddington to Exeter St David's via Bristol on 7 June. *Brian Morrison/TG*

TWYFORD (2): This view, looking towards Paddington, shows the station following the introduction of the first BR DMUs. By the time of the second visit, in October 1998, these units had been withdrawn from passenger service, so it was difficult to comprehend the sight of one of these units approaching from Reading. This is No L842 of Class 101, which is used with an additional centre coach ('Iris') by the BR Laboratory at Derby. *C. L. Caddy/TG*

TWYFORD (3): These are the local lines in the 1960s looking towards Reading. The bay for the Henley-on-Thames trains is in the right background beyond the footbridge.

A few hours spent at Twyford produces a surprising variety of trains. I had just decided to catch the approaching DMU to Reading on the morning of 15 October 1998 when I heard the characteristic sound of a Class 37 diesel on the up line, and No 37375 passed through the station with a train of London Underground stock. *C. L. Caddy/TG*

TWYFORD (4): The branch was opened from Twyford to Henley-on-Thames in 1857, with one intermediate station at Shiplake; both these stations are in Oxfordshire (see *British Railways Past and Present No 15*). On 14 December 1985 single-car DMU No 120 of Class 121 (vehicle No W55020), in chocolate and cream livery, forms the branch train. The present-day service is usually worked by Class 165 units; in the 'present' picture, taken in June 2001, it is No 165129. *C. L. Caddy/TG*

WARGRAVE station, which is only 1¾ miles from Twyford, was not opened until the branch was 43 years old. The first view shows the station on 15 May 1966, and although the line had been singled by this time, the GWR building on the up side was still in use.

A visit in October 1998 revealed that the original buildings had gone, to be replaced by a small open shelter. Trees have encroached over the old down trackbed, so that it is no longer obvious that this was once a double-track line. *C. L. Caddy/TG*

REDISCOVERING RAILWAYS

READING GENERAL (1): A heavy freight train from the SR makes an impressive sight approaching Reading behind Class N No 31809 in January 1963. The WR General station is behind the camera and the SR station to the right.

The same location is now much tidier but less interesting. The Brighton to Preston mail train behind Class 47 No 47600 approaches Reading on the afternoon of 23 March 1993. The electrified lines on the extreme right are for the SR trains to Waterloo, and are also used by the Redhill and Gatwick DMU trains. *Chris Gammell/TG*

BERKSHIRE

READING GENERAL (2): Class 5700 No 4661 approaches Reading with a down freight train on 26 April 1958. Freight trains still regularly pass through Reading, and on 23 March 1993 Class 33 No 33065 works an afternoon ballast train. The platforms for trains from the former SR terminating at Reading are immediately behind the camera. *Great Western Trust, courtesy Laurence Waters/TG*

READING GENERAL (3): A visit in October 1998 saw Railtrack service unit No 930004 entering the SR island platform. This is a Sandite and de-icing unit, in this instance being used for leaf-clearing. The vehicles were formerly Nos 10907 and 10908 from 4SUB No 4361, which was withdrawn in 1974. On 7 June 2001 the 16.33 Paddington to Penzance train was hauled by Class 47 No 47816 *Bristol Bath Road Quality Approved*. On the right is the 16.56 to Waterloo via Hounslow. *Both TG*

READING GENERAL (4): 'Manor' Class No 7817 *Garsington Manor* is on station pilot duties on 5 August 1963. This bay platform is at the London end of Reading station and is currently used by some local trains to and from Paddington.

On 20 June 2001 the bay is occupied by Class 165 No 165131, which will leave for Paddington at 10.04 on a stopping service. On the right a Virgin Cross Country train, the 06.10 from Manchester Piccadilly, has just arrived. It will reverse, before proceeding to Poole. The power unit is Class 43 No 43068. *Great Western Trust (Derek Tuck), courtesy Laurence Waters/TG*

READING GENERAL (5): An up freight train passes through the station in dismal weather on 12 January 1953, hauled by 'Dukedog' Class No 9015.

On 19 June 2001 a Class 47 is on the 06.30 Plymouth to Paddington train, and significant changes are apparent in both motive power and the station buildings. The station has been rebuilt and a footbridge added; the original main buildings on the down side have been retained, but are no longer part of the station. The clock tower of the main building is illustrated on page 46. *R. C. Riley/TG*

READING (WR) MPD (1) had an allocation of about 100 steam locomotives in early BR days. By the time this photograph was taken in 1964 the number of steam engines had dropped to 15, as diesel locomotives increasingly took over.

These in turn have been almost completely displaced by DMUs, and this is the same location in April 1993. The MPD has been replaced by what is referred to as the Reading Turbo Maintenance Depot, and even first-generation DMUs are outnumbered by the then recently introduced 'Thames Turbos'. The units are, from left to right, Nos L594, 165104, Departmental DMUs 97775/6 (the ATP Test Development & Training Unit), 165107 and 165101. *Philip J. Kelley/TG*

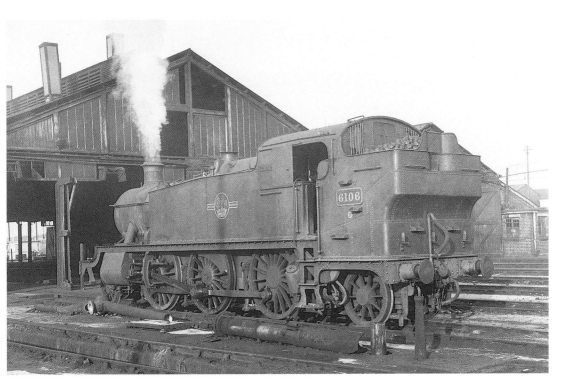

READING (WR) DEPOT (2) was given the code 81D by BR. Here Class 6100 No 6106 waits on shed for its next duty. Members of this class were extensively used in the London area.

The shed buildings and other attributes have been swept away and the site is now used for the berthing and maintenance of DMUs and engineers' vehicles. This is the view from the Reading-Reading West line on 19 April 1993. *Great Western Trust, courtesy Laurence Waters/TG*

LINES FROM WATERLOO

Windsor branch

WINDSOR & ETON RIVERSIDE: Steam was rarely seen on passenger trains at Windsor in BR days, but on 23 June 1957 the author travelled from Surbiton to Windsor behind 'Remembrance' Class No 32331 *Beattie*. This is the special ready for the return journey to Waterloo, taken by another photographer. In the station is a normal service train consisting of an SR 4COR unit.

Much of the station has been redeveloped and sold for office use. However, part of the overall roof has been retained, together with two platforms. On 5 May 1999 Class 455 No 5713 leaves the station forming the 08.44 service to Waterloo. *David Lawrence, courtesy Hugh Davies/TG*

LINES FROM WATERLOO
Ascot to Bracknell

ASCOT (1): A record of two very different trains at Ascot. The first photograph shows a railway enthusiasts' special on 23 March 1963, which had started the day at Farnborough and toured secondary lines in Hampshire and Berkshire. Class M7 No 30108 was used throughout the day.

On 20 June 2001 newly commissioned Class 458 No 8008 has just arrived on the 12.27 from Guildford, which terminates at Ascot. The left-face of this island platform is no longer in use. *Both TG*

ASCOT (2): Heavy freight trains were marshalled at Feltham and those for the Western Region could be seen passing through Ascot. On 19 May 1962 a Class S15 approaches on its way to Reading.

Those days are now over and the only long trains guaranteed to be seen are the annual special passenger trains bringing visitors to the Races. On 19 June 2001 Class 47 No 47725 *The Railway Mission* enters Ascot on a race special from Victoria. On the extreme right is Class 73 No 73109 *Battle of Britain 50th Anniversary*. *Both TG*

Other interesting workings occasionally arise because of engineering works on the main line between Paddington and Reading. On 30 October 1992 stone empties returning to the Mendips were routed through Ascot, and this train is hauled by Class 59 No 59102. *TG*

ASCOT (3) is also the junction for the line from Guildford, and coming off this line on 19 May 1962 is Class N No 31858 with a solitary SR brake-van.

On 30 October 1992 Sandite unit No 930015 has reached Ascot by the same route. Here it reversed before continuing to Reading. The coaches are from a Class 4EPB built in 1953. *Both TG*

ASCOT (4): Class 2HAP (414) No 4319 has just left Ascot and takes the sharp curve for Aldershot on 21 May 1991; the Reading line is in the foreground. This is the 08.38 from Staines, and on arrival at Aldershot it will reverse and continue to Guildford. All these units have since been withdrawn and the service is worked by 4VEPs and 458s.

On 17 June 1999 a Races special is also taking this line; it is the 19.09 from Ascot to Waterloo, which is 'top and tailed' by Class 73 electro-diesels, the rear locomotive being No 73110. *Both TG*

REDISCOVERING RAILWAYS

MARTINS HERON: In the days when Feltham and Nine Elms yards were open there was a succession of freight trains to Reading and thence on to the WR. On a misty November morning in 1963 Class S15 No 30837 works a freight from Feltham near Ascot.

During 1988 a new station, known as Martins Heron, was opened between Ascot and Bracknell. By pure chance the 'past' photograph was taken close to the site of the new station, which is seen on 23 March 1993. *Both TG*

BRACKNELL: Class N No 31819 works light through Bracknell on its way to Guildford shed on 19 May 1962. The station was later rebuilt, but is no more attractive in its present form. Class 4CIG (421) No 1305 forms a Reading to Waterloo train on 30 October 1992. *Both TG*

LINES FROM WATERLOO AND GUILDFORD

Sandhurst Halt to Reading

SANDHURST HALT: Sandhurst is on the boundary of three counties, Hampshire, Surrey and Berkshire, the halt itself being in Berkshire. Approaching the halt on 25 May 1963 is BR Standard Class 4MT No 75070 with the 11.05am train from Reading. Semaphore signals were used on most of the line, but this section was controlled by colour light signals, as seen in the background.

The signals here have gone, although the whole line now has colour light signals. On 4 June 1998 the 16.38 semi-fast Reading to Gatwick Airport via Redhill service, formed of Class 165 No 165122, passes through Sandhurst. The journey time from Reading to Redhill is 1 hour. *Both TG*

CROWTHORNE (1): On 25 May 1963 Class U No 31624 leaves Crowthorne on the ex-SECR Reading to Redhill line with the 12.05pm from Reading. The train consists of narrow-bodied Maunsell coaches built for the Hastings line.

As at so many stations, the yard has been sold and is used in this instance by a plant hire company. No L594, a 'Cross Country' unit of Class 119, works the 10.33 Reading to Gatwick Airport service on 30 September 1992. *Both TG*

CROWTHORNE (2): Standard Class 4MT No 80137 stops at Crowthorne on the 12.18pm Reading to Redhill train on 25 May 1963. This was an all-stations train (except Earley, Winnersh Halt and Wanborough), and took 1¾ hours to reach Redhill.

In addition to trains starting from Reading there are now a few from further afield. The service from Liverpool Lime Street (11.35) to Portsmouth Harbour is operated by Virgin Trains using two-coach DMUs, which on occasions are grossly overcrowded. This is Class 158 No 158751 on 4 June 1998. *Both TG*

SOUTHERN RAILWAY.
CROWTHORNE
The holder is prohibited from entering the Companies' Trains. Not Transferable
Admit ONE to PLATFORM 1D.
AVAILABLE ONE HOUR.
This Ticket must be given up on leaving Platform.
FOR CONDITIONS SEE BACK

WOKINGHAM is where the SECR and LSWR lines to Reading converge. On 6 June 1964 Class S15 No 30824 passes the 1.35pm Redhill to Reading train, behind Class N No 31408. The junction signals can be seen in the background.

On 21 February 2002 recently introduced Class 220 No 220022 forms the 14.40 Portsmouth & Southsea to Blackpool North service. The station has been rebuilt and there is an additional overbridge between the two platforms. The footbridge in the background is for public access across the railway when the level crossing barriers are closed. *Edwin Wilmshurst/TG*

WINNERSH HALT (1) on 29 May 1965 sees a pair of two-car SR electric units forming the 2.54pm Waterloo to Reading train. The units are 2BILs, Nos 2027 and 2048.

New facilities have been provided at Winnersh, and on 23 March 1993 Class 117 DMU No L410 pulls away from the station forming the 15.10 Reading to Redhill service. This is the first Redhill train of the day to stop at Winnersh – only Waterloo trains normally stop here. *Michael Mensing/TG*

_(1/39) SOUTHERN RAILWAY.

———

(787)

FROM WATERLOO TO

WINNERSH HALT

WINNERSH HALT (2): A Reading to Redhill train passes through Winnersh behind Class U No 31625 in the late 1950s. There were separate entrances for the up and down platforms, approached from a road overbridge behind the camera.

A Waterloo train, the 12.26 from Reading, is seen passing Winnersh on 15 October 1998. Winnersh has a half-hourly stopping service to Waterloo, which leaves Reading a few minutes after the fast trains. *David Lawrence, courtesy Hugh Davies/TG*

EARLEY: A first-generation DMU stops at Earley forming the 07.46 all-stations Guildford to Reading service on 21 May 1991. The unit is No L841 of Class 101.

Network Turbos progressively replaced these DMUs on this route from the winter of 1993. Services are now worked by Class 165 units, in this instance No 165002, which on 15 October 1998 is forming the 13.35 Reading to Gatwick Airport train. *Both TG*

London and South Western Ry.

787

TO

EARLEY

Left READING SOUTHERN (1): The SR terminus at Reading was known as Reading Southern and later Reading South. The approach as seen from a train window shows the almost empty motive power depot and derelict yard towards the end of the steam era. The embankment to the right carries the WR main line from Paddington.

The whole area occupied by the SR has been redeveloped and this is the site once occupied by the locomotive yard, as seen on 24 March 1993. *Ray Ruffell, courtesy Laurence Waters/TG*

READING SOUTHERN (2): The size of the SR facilities at Reading can be judged from this photograph taken from the WR main line on 25 March 1956. The locomotive shed is on the extreme right and the goods yards in the background. The running roads into Reading SR pass in front of the signal box, and the lines in the foreground connect the SR and WR.

Today the site is occupied by a large office block and car parks. Clues to the alignment are the line in the foreground and its fencing, and in the left background the church tower with its four turrets. *Both TG*

READING SOUTHERN (3): On 24 October 1964 Class U No 31639 acts as station pilot in the SR station, which closed in September 1965. All SR trains now use new bay platforms at Reading WR, the platform canopies of which can be glimpsed on the right. The other clue to the location is the distant clock tower of the Western Region station. Today there is no indication that there was ever a second station here. *Hugh Ballantyne/TG*

READING SOUTHERN (4): On the last day of official steam passenger train haulage (3 January 1965), Class Q No 30545 enters Reading Southern station on a special train. To the left is the SR locomotive shed, and beyond can be seen signals on the WR main line from Paddington.

A view from the same point today shows how radical have been the changes since the SR site was closed. Apart from new buildings, the railway bridge has been removed and the roads realigned. *Great Western Trust, courtesy Laurence Waters/TG*

SOUTHERN RAILWAY.

Issued subject to the Bye-laws, Regulations and Conditions in the Company's Bills and Notices.

READING

The holder is prohibited from entering the Company's Trains. Not Transferable.

Admit ONE to Platform 1d.

AVAILABLE ONE HOUR ON DAY OF ISSUE ONLY.
This Ticket must be given up on leaving Platform

READING (SR) MPD (1): 'West Country' Class No 34037 *Clovelly* graces the shed on 15 December 1963. The GWR main line is on the left, and the SR terminus some distance behind the camera. The gas works is visible in the background beyond the shed.

Redevelopment of the site makes exact location of the spot difficult, but a gap in the industrial buildings that now occupy the former SR territory enables an almost matching view to be obtained. The signals controlling the WR main line, and the gas holder in the background, confirm the location in March 1994. *Hugh Ballantyne/TG*

READING (SR) MPD (2): At the back of the shed on 27 June 1959 Class E1 No 31497 has been dumped. This was a Bricklayers Arms engine, so it is not clear why it was at Reading. It was later stored at Ashford and scrapped in November 1960.

The present-day view shows a Waterloo train in the additional platform that was built at Reading WR following the closure of the SR station. *R. C. Riley/TG*

READING TO BASINGSTOKE

MORTIMER on 27 November 1976 sees Class 52 No 1010 *Western Campaigner* **working a special train towards Basingstoke.**

The station is still open and an unnumbered first-generation DMU forms the 11.50 Reading to Basingstoke train. Almost all services had been taken over by 'Thames Turbos' at the beginning of the 1993 summer service, a week earlier. *D. E. Canning/TG*

MAIN LINES WEST OF READING

Reading to Goring troughs

TILEHURST (1) is the first station west of Reading on the WR main line. In the 1960s, BR Standards of the 'Britannia' Class were used on many of the expresses from South Wales, and here is No 70025 *Western Star* heading the 'Red Dragon' on 17 September 1955.

Tilehurst has changed little, and on 5 June 2001 a Class 47 passes the same point on the 09.09 Virgin Trains service from Manchester Piccadilly to Paddington. *R. C. Riley/TG*

TILEHURST (2): Class 4300 No 7317 is seen on the up local line on 7 July 1956 with a through train to the SR, while on 7 June 2001, seen from the other side of the lines, an up freight train is double-headed by Class 57s Nos 57002 and 57009. *R. C. Riley/TG*

PANGBOURNE (1): The 'past' photograph of Pangbourne station and local lines is looking towards Paddington, and despite the passage of a century or so few changes have been made to this part of the station. Out of view on the right are the remains of the platforms for the up and down main lines, as a down Freightliner passes on 15 April 1999, hauled by Class 47 No 47345. *Lens of Sutton/TG*

PANGBOURNE (2): An inter-regional train from the North East to Bournemouth approaches the station on 17 September 1955 hauled by 'King Arthur' Class No 30742 *Camelot*. An express passenger train code is displayed, but not the Southern Region code with which the locomotive would be more familiar.

The modern scene on the morning of 15 April 1999 is represented by an InterCity 125 forming the 11.00 Paddington to Swansea service, and a freight train hauled by Class 58 No 58016. *R. C. Riley/TG*

GORING TROUGHS (1) represent the last point of interest on the main line before it leaves Berkshire. In the 'past' picture a down freight train hauled by Class 2800 No 2898 is seen there in the early 1960s.

The troughs have been removed, but the scene has otherwise hardly changed over the decades. On 21 February 2002 Class 66 No 66650 takes a train of cars and vans from Southampton West Docks to Crewe. *Hugh Ballantyne/TG*

GORING TROUGHS (2): Class N No 31401 heads toward Reading and the Southern Region on a heavy freight train in the early 1960s. Some 40 years later, a Class 220 'Voyager' passes the same point forming the 06.20 Edinburgh-Bournemouth service. *Hugh Ballantyne/TG*

MAIN LINES WEST OF READING

Reading to Hungerford

READING WEST (1) is seen here in the 1960s; the train in the right background beyond Oxford Road Junction is heading for Reading General, the WR main-line station, while the line to the left joins the main line west of General.

The motive power depot is situated in the triangle so formed. Just south of the station, at Southcote Junction, the Basingstoke and Berks & Hants lines meet.

Today a new DMU depot occupies the vee of Oxford Road Junction. Class 47 No 47806 is hauling the 06.50 Edinburgh to Bournemouth on 24 May 2001; because this train was running over an hour late, it omitted its scheduled stop at Reading and was instead routed via the west curve. *R. C. Riley/TG*

READING WEST (2): An inter-regional train negotiates Oxford Road Junction on its way to Basingstoke in 1962, hauled by 'Grange' Class No 6879 *Overton Grange*. Today Paddington to Plymouth trains are normally formed of HST units, but on 16 March 1999 the 16.35 from Paddington was hauled by a Class 47 in GWR-style green livery. *D. E. Canning/TG*

Left GWR platform ticket 6058 issued from the up office

READING WEST (3): A light load for Class 2251 No 3219, seen entering Reading West from Newbury on 30 July 1960. Another light load was seen on the morning of 13 September 1999 when an unidentified Class 37 hauled a few ballast hopper wagons towards the engineer's yard at Reading. *Great Western Trust, courtesy Laurence Waters/TG*

Right GWR platform ticket 9290 issued from the down office

READING WEST (D) 9290

G.W.RLY. S.3

The holder is prohibited from entering the Company's Trains. Not Transferable.

Admit ONE to PLATFORM 1D Available ONE HOUR on DAY of ISSUE ONLY.

This ticket must be given up on leaving Platform.

FOR CONDITIONS SEE BACK

READING WEST (4): 'West Country' Class No 34102 *Lapford* of Bournemouth shed enters Reading West on an inter-regional train in 1962. Duty 401 was a Bournemouth to Weymouth return trip, and although not recorded at the time, this is almost certainly the daily Bournemouth to Birkenhead train. It stopped at Reading West because it took the Oxford Road to West Junction spur, thereby bypassing Reading (General).

Virgin Cross Country trains now provide a south-to-north service and most run via Reading (General) where they reverse. Heavy freight trains also frequently pass through Reading West, and in September 1999 Class 59 No 59101 *Village of Whatley* hauls a massive stone train from Merehead to Acton. *D. E. Canning/TG*

SOUTHCOTE JUNCTION, just south of Reading West, is readily accessible by a public footpath that gives good views of trains on both the Basingstoke and Newbury lines. On 4 July 1959 'Castle' Class No 7022 *Hereford Castle* approaches the junction (the line on the right is not the Basingstoke line, but a spur to Central Goods).

The Central Goods line has been taken up, but the other two lines are heavily used by both passenger and freight trains. On 17 March 1994 Class 37 No 37042 takes a ballast train to Westbury. *R. C. Riley/TG*

THEALE is the first station on the Berks & Hants line beyond Southcote Junction. From the junction to the boundary with Wiltshire, the railway, the A4 trunk road and the Kennet & Avon Canal run parallel. Here a 'Western' Class diesel-hydraulic locomotive speeds through the station with a passenger train bound for Paddington in 1969.

In May 1993 an 'Intercity 125' passes through the station forming the 09.42 Penzance to Paddington service. The footbridge has not only been renewed but also relocated adjacent to the road bridge. *D. E. Canning/TG*

ALDERMASTON was the scene of track relaying on 23 March 1975. The diesel shunter is Ruston & Hornsby No PWM 653, later Class 97/6 No 97653.

In 1993 'Thames Turbo' No 165110 arrives with the 12.27 stopping service from Newbury to Paddington. *D. E. Canning/TG*

MIDGHAM: A down ballast train worked by Class 52 No 1059 *Western Enterprise* stands at the level crossing in 1969.

On 21 May 1993 the modern image is represented by an empty stone train from Acton returning to Merehead Quarry hauled by Foster Yeoman Class 59 No 59005 *Kenneth J. Painter*, and seen from the other side of the line. The notices in the two photographs both warn against trespassing, the present one being much more economical with its wording! *D. E. Canning/TG*

THATCHAM (1) is seen first in the 1950s, surrounded by particularly ugly industrial development. There is little improvement in 2001, although the modern station buildings are in much better condition than the old GWR buildings. A train of empty wagons heads for Westbury hauled by a Class 59. *Stewart Wise/TG*

THATCHAM (2): A 1960s excursion from Ramsgate is taking an unusual route along the Berks & Hants line to its final destination of Paignton, hauled by a Class 33. Note the absence of station buildings and footbridge.

Another locomotive-hauled passenger train, this time behind a Class 47, passes through Thatcham on 20 June 2001 forming the 15.33 Paddington to Penzance service, and viewed from the re-instated footbridge. *D. E. Canning/TG*

THATCHAM (3): 'King' Class No 6021 *King Richard II* pounds through Thatcham towards Paddington on a train from Ilfracombe (12.25pm) and Minehead (2.15pm) on 30 July 1960.

Today nothing as grand regularly passes through Thatcham, and normal passenger trains are either HSTs or DMUs such as this Class 165, No 165101, which is working the 11.00 Newbury to Reading service on 15 October 1998.
Great Western Trust, courtesy Laurence Waters/TG

NEWBURY RACECOURSE was only normally opened on race days, when a succession of special trains would arrive. Here 'Castle' Class No 5074 *Hampden* passes 'King' Class No 6010 *King Charles I*, both on 1st Class-only Members' race trains on 5 March 1960.

The station was opened on a regular basis in 1988 and has an hourly service on weekdays; all passenger trains now use the platforms on the extreme left. On 12 March 1993 an 'Intercity 125' forms the up 'Cornish Riviera' express. In recent years small industrial units have been built on the up side adjacent to the station. *R. C. Riley/TG*

NEWBURY (1): The station, in the centre of the town, was the junction for the Lambourn branch (which closed on 4 January 1960) and the former Didcot, Newbury & Southampton Railway (DNSR) lines. Almost every line is occupied in this photograph of the station taken on 24 February 1939. Class 2301 No 2535 shunts in the Lambourn bay on the extreme left, while 'Duke' Class No 3280 takes a DNSR train on the down through line. In the down platform 'Star' Class No 4038 *Queen Berengaria* is on a Weymouth train. In the down side bay 'Hall' Class No 5950 *Wardley Hall* is on a stopping train to Devizes.

On 7 July 1956 'Hall' Class No 6910 *Gossington Hall* heads west with a troop train, while an ex-GWR railcar can just be glimpsed beneath the platform canopy on the left, forming the Lambourn train.

Today Newbury has lost the up and down bays and the signal box, but the main station buildings have been retained. On 17 March 1999 a scene from the 1970s was relived when Class 31 No 31203 hauled a train of traditional-style open wagons from West Drayton to Westbury. *Great Western Trust, courtesy Laurence Waters/R. C. Riley/ TG*

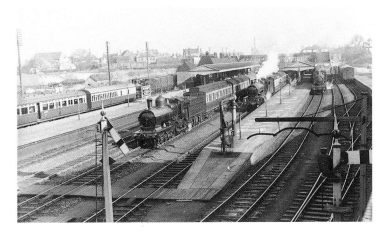

NEWBURY (2): With the station in the distance beyond the road overbridge, a train of oil tankers leaves Newbury behind BR Standard Class 9F No 92150.

Heavy freight can still be seen, with the frequent passage of stone trains to and from the Mendips. On 17 March 1999 a train of empty wagons passes the same spot, hauled as usual by a member of Class 59. *D. E. Canning/TG*

ENBORNE JUNCTION: This photograph, taken in 1961 and showing an up express train, is looking west towards Enborne Junction, the signals for which are just visible beyond the rear coach.

In the spring of 1999 the same location has lost its junction, but in its place is an overbridge carrying the controversial and recently opened Newbury Bypass. The up stone train is hauled by Class 59 No 59102 *Village of Chantry*. *D. E. Canning/TG*

KINTBURY (1): A Reading-bound train enters Kintbury on 29 May 1976 formed of Class 117 DMU No L425. Something altogether more impressive fills the viewfinder at the same spot on 15 April 1999, as Class 59 No 59103, in its new livery, takes a train-load of stone hoppers from Merehead to Acton. *C. L. Caddy/TG*

KINTBURY (2): This view was taken from the up platform looking west on 24 February 1965. Modernisation subsequently came to Kintbury, as the 1999 photograph shows; the train is the 09.48 Bedwyn to Paddington, formed of Class 166 No 166216 on 15 April. *C. L. Caddy/TG*

HUNGERFORD (1): The railway and canal are very close together between Kintbury and Hungerford, as can be seen in this photograph at Hungerford Common, with 'Warship' Class No D809 *Champion* working the 16.30 Paddington to Plymouth and Kingswear train on 29 May 1965.

On 10 March 1994 an empty ARC stone train hauled by Class 59 No 59102 *Village of Chantry* makes an impressive sight as it heads west past the same point. *Michael Mensing/TG*

HUNGERFORD (2) is host to Class 52 No 1057 *Western Chieftain* on a westbound train in 1970. There is little evidence of much local traffic, as the car park is almost deserted.

The view in 1993 makes an interesting contrast, with 'Thames Turbo' No 165122 entering the rebuilt station on the evening of 21 May. The unit is working the 17.43 service from Reading to Bedwyn, the latter being the next station, which is in Wiltshire. Hungerford is now regarded as part of the commuter area, as indicated by the significant number of cars outside the station. *D. E. Canning/TG*

DIDCOT, NEWBURY & SOUTHAMPTON LINE

ENBORNE JUNCTION: The first station on the DNSR line southwards from Newbury was at Woodhay, just over the county boundary, and the line closed completely at the end of 1962. Class 9F No 92231 has just left the main line at Enborne Junction and is heading for Eastleigh in 1961; the signals protecting the junction can be seen in the background.

   All that remains of the line at this point is a depression in the field and a gap in the hedgerow where the junction was once situated. A Class 165 DMU passes the site of the junction in March 1999. *D. E. Canning/TG*

HERMITAGE was the first station northwards after the DNSR line left the GWR main line at Newbury East Junction, between Newbury Racecourse and Newbury stations. This section of the line closed to passengers in September 1962 and to freight two years later. The station is seen here on 23 July 1962, with a single-car DMU on an afternoon train from Didcot. Towards the end of the line's life there were only four trains per day in each direction.

Like many of the DNSR stations, Hermitage is now a private house, while the trackbed immediately to the south of the station has disappeared under a field. *Chris Gammell/TG*

PINEWOOD HALT was only three-quarters of a mile north of Hermitage, and is seen here on 16 December 1961 looking towards Didcot. The bridge still exists today, but the trackbed in the immediate vicinity has been used to dump surplus earth. Beyond this pile the land has been cleared and laid out as a public park. *Edwin Wilmshurst/TG*

HAMPSTEAD NORRIS is seen here in the summer of 1962. The station was approached by a short steep hill to the left where the chimneys of old house can be seen. A road passes under the railway at the far end of the station.

A visit in the spring of 1993 revealed that the area has completely changed; there is now no trace of the station, and the overbridge and part of the embankment have been removed. This is the view from Station Hill, and today houses, behind the camera, occupy the station site. The house in the centre of the photograph is approximately in the position of the starting signal in the distance in the 'past' photograph, and the embankment, which is still in place behind this house, is at the first-floor level. *Chris Gammell/TG*

REDISCOVERING RAILWAYS

COMPTON: A southbound train consisting of a Bulleid set hauled by Class 2251 No 2246 leaves Compton in the late 1950s.

Trains were operated by DMUs towards the end, and on 23 July 1962 a single-car unit stops at Compton on its way to Newbury.

There is nothing left of the station today, as the third view from the same point shows; the station approach and the area surrounding the station are now within a school. *David Lawrence, courtesy Hugh Davies/Chris Gammell/TG*

LAMBOURN BRANCH

NEWBURY WEST JUNCTION: A special train of DMUs takes the Lambourn branch out of Newbury. The Lambourn line was removed in 1976. The same location today shows the remains of the branch embankment covered in trees as Class 37 No 37216 heads west on the main line with a ballast train on 17 March 1999. *D. E. Canning/TG*

NEWBURY WEST FIELDS HALT: Just beyond this halt the Lambourn branch crossed the Kennet & Avon Canal, and to mark complete closure of the line a DMU made several trips on the branch as far as Welford Park on 3 November 1973; this is one such working.

The bridge has since been removed, but the abutments and embankment are still in place, as seen in this 1999 view. *D. E. Canning/TG*

STOCKCROSS & BAGNOR: River, road and railway ran parallel along the Lambourn Valley, and numerous halts and small stations served the villages along the branch. This is Stockcross & Bagnor, 2½ miles from Newbury, looking towards Lambourn in late 1959.

The line is now difficult to locate and all that remains are the abutments of what was once a railway bridge over a narrow lane. It is this that confirms the identity of the two locations. The waiting shelter, however, has survived and is now located at the Great Western Society's Centre at Didcot. *Chris Gammell/TG*

REDISCOVERING RAILWAYS

BOXFORD was another rudimentary station. A train bound for Lambourn is about to leave in this December 1959 view.

The station approach road still exists and is now used as the private drive to a house. The station was located in the garden and this is the present-day matching view, identified by the older houses in the background (and by the owner of the house). From here too the waiting shelter has survived and in a much modified form serves as the village bus shelter. *Chris Gammell/TG*

WELFORD PARK: An unrealistic air of activity is generated by two engines at Welford Park on 19 September 1959. This location achieved some importance in the 1950s when a line was built from here to a nearby United States military establishment, which was used until 1972. Class 5700 No 7708 arrives with the 5.20pm from Newbury, to which Class 2251 No 2252 is returning light engine.

The station has been demolished, but the platforms were clearly visible in 1993. The booking office exists at the Great Western Society's Centre at Didcot. *Hugh Ballantyne/TG*

GREAT SHEFFORD: There are parcels and Lyons cakes but no passengers in the winter of 1959. Today it is hard to detect that there was ever a railway here. Part of the station site is occupied by new houses, and beyond them are fields, as shown in this 1993 view. The curve of the field and the trees across the background are the only identifying features. *Chris Gammell/TG*

EASTBURY was another basic halt serving the adjacent village and nearby farms. This view is looking towards Lambourn.

The footpath along the side of the railway is still in use and the other marker to link the two views is the house below the embankment. *Chris Gammell/TG*

LAMBOURN (1): Unlike many branch-line termini, Lambourn station was conveniently situated on the edge of the town. Class 5700 No 7788 with a single-coach train waits to leave for Newbury on 1 February 1958.

The same view in 1993 is readily identified by the hut behind the water crane at the buffer-stop end of the station. The yard is occupied by industrial buildings and a house has been erected in the field beyond the station. *Chris Gammell/TG*

LAMBOURN (2): Class 2251 No 2252 has just arrived on the 4.10pm from Newbury on 19 September 1959. The trees on the left of the 'present' view mark the position of the station building and the sheds on the right are on the site of the run-round loop and goods yard. *Hugh Ballantyne/TG*

GAZETTEER OF BERKSHIRE'S RAILWAYS

Mileages are taken from the Western and Southern Region Passenger Services Timetables, 11 September 1961, where possible. Stations were opened and closed on the same dates as their respective lines unless otherwise stated. Some opening dates refer to the first appearance of the station in the public timetable.

GWR lines from Paddington

Windsor branch

Station in Berkshire (1960s boundaries): Windsor & Eton Central (2¾m).

Opening and closure: Line opened 8.10.1849. Windsor & Eton rebuilt 1883-84 and renamed Windsor & Eton Central in 1.1950.

Route and traffic: The branch leaves Slough on a sharp curve, continuing south-west over open country before reaching a long viaduct that carries the line over the River Thames into Berkshire. This is immediately followed by a sharp curve to the east as the line enters Windsor. The line is now dissected by overbridges carrying the M4 motorway and a dual carriageway just south of the site of Chalvey Halt. The line was built mainly for passenger traffic and in particular for Royal Trains. Normal passenger trains were operated by motor-trains or diesel railcars. It currently has a very frequent DMU service, a high proportion of passengers being tourists.

Bourne End branch

Stations in Berkshire (1960s boundaries): Furze Platt Halt (1¼m from Maidenhead), Cookham (3m); other stations in Buckinghamshire.

Opening and closure: Line opened 1.8.1854. The first station on the branch, just after the junction, was called Maidenhead (Boyne Hill); it was called Maidenhead (Wycombe Branch) to about 1866 and closed 1.11.1871. Furze Platt Halt opened 5.7.1937.

Route and traffic: The line leaves Maidenhead on a sharp curve and runs north through what was open country to Cookham, after which it crosses the River Thames into Buckinghamshire. The only gradient of note is 1 in 84 at Cookham. Furze Platt was built to serve a new housing development. There were some through trains to Aylesbury until closure of the line north of Bourne End. The line has played an increasing role in transporting commuters to Maidenhead, London and Reading and it currently enjoys a very frequent service (which runs to Marlow, with a reversal at Bourne End).

Main Line to Reading

Stations in Berkshire (1960s boundaries): Maidenhead (24¼m from Paddington), Twyford (31m), Reading (36m).

Opening and closure: Taplow to Twyford opened 1.7.1839 and Twyford to Reading 30.3.1840. Taplow opened as Maidenhead; the present Maidenhead station opened when the line was extended to Reading. Reading was rebuilt in 1868 and again in 1898/99, 1965 and 1986/89, officially re-opening 4.4.1989. Reading became Reading General in 11.1949 and reverted to Reading in 5.1973.

Route and traffic: After passing through Taplow (Bucks), the railway crosses the River Thames and enters Berkshire. There are gentle curves at both Maidenhead and Reading, otherwise a straight run with negligible gradients, enabling high speeds to be maintained. Between Twyford and Reading is Sonning Cutting. Traffic is mainly passenger, both long-distance and local. There is also a substantial amount of freight even to the present day. There were extensive freight yards at Reading and the railway received much business from local factories. The goods depot at the east end of the station (and the original factories) have been closed. For connections with the SER and its successors see below under 'Guildford to Reading'.

Henley-on-Thames branch

Station in Berkshire (1960s boundaries): Wargrave (1¾m from Twyford); other stations in Oxfordshire.

Opening and closure: Line opened 1.6.1857. Wargrave opened 1.10.1900.

Route and traffic: On leaving Twyford the line immediately turns north, the only gradient of note being 1 in 70 at Wargrave. Shortly beyond Wargrave the line crosses the River Thames, which marks the county boundary. Trains were operated by motor-trains or diesel railcars. There is currently a frequent service provided by DMUs.

Lines from Waterloo and Guildford

Windsor branch (LSWR)

Station in Berkshire (1960s boundaries): Windsor & Eton Riverside (25¾m from Waterloo and 6¾m from junction at Staines). Other stations on the branch were in Middlesex and Buckinghamshire.

Opening and closure: Line opened from Datchet to Windsor 1.12.1849.

Windsor & Eton Riverside opened as Windsor and was renamed Windsor & Eton 10.12.1903. The suffix Riverside was added at Nationalisation. Line electrified 6.7.1930.

Route and traffic: The line runs north-west from Staines over the flat land of Staines Moor and Datchet Common, before crossing the River Thames into Berkshire as the line begins its almost 180-degree turn into Windsor. The line served the small communities at intermediate points, but most importantly Windsor itself. It

still performs these functions and there is considerable commuter and leisure traffic.

Waterloo to Bracknell (LSWR) and Wokingham

Stations in Berkshire: Ascot (29m from Waterloo), Ascot West (29¼m), Martins Heron (31¼m), Bracknell (32¼m), Wokingham (36¾m – see entry below in 'Guildford to Reading' section).

Opening and closure: The line opened between Ascot and Wokingham 9.7.1856. Ascot opened 4.6.1856 and Ascot West in 1922 for the racecourse; it closed in 1965. Martins Heron opened 16.5.1988. Bracknell was rebuilt in 1976. The line was electrified from Ascot to Wokingham and Reading South 1.1.1939. The line from Ascot to Ash Vale opened 18.3.1878 to Sturt Lane and to Ash Vale 2.6.1879. It was electrified 1.1.1939.

Route and traffic: The line enters Berkshire just beyond Sunningdale and passes through what used to be a sparsely populated area. All this has changed and housing development has resulted in a huge increase in the number of passengers. Bracknell was designated a New Town after the Second World War. An intermediate station has been opened to serve more recent housing estates. The racecourse at Ascot also attracts passengers, some brought from distant parts by special trains.

Guildford to Reading (SER)

Stations in Berkshire: Sandhurst Halt (14¼m from Guildford), Crowthorne (15¾m), Wokingham (19m from Guildford and 36¾m from Waterloo via Ascot), Winnersh Halt (21m and 38¾m), Winnersh Triangle (21½m and 39¼m), Earley (22¾m and 40½m), Reading Southern (25¾m and 43½m).

Crowthorne was named Wellington College until 17.6.1928. Winnersh Halt opened as Sindlesham & Hurst Halt and was renamed 6.7.1930. Reading Southern was called Reading until 26.9.1949, then Reading South until 11.9.1961.

Opening and closure: The line opened 4.7.1849. Sandhurst Halt opened in 6.1852, closed 12.1853, and re-opened 1909. Crowthorne opened 29.1.1859 and was re-sited a few years later. Winnersh Halt opened 1.1.1910, Winnersh Triangle 11.5.1987 and Earley 11.1863. Reading was re-sited 30.8.1855 and rebuilt in 1860. A connection to the GWR opened on 1.12.1858 (for goods) and 17.1.1859 (passengers). Another line connecting the two railways opened 17.12.1899 (closed 4.4.1965), and yet another connecting spur opened 26.5.1941. The last change was 6.9.1965 when all trains from the Southern Region were diverted to a new platform at Reading (General). At the same time Reading Southern was closed. Another platform for SR trains was added at Reading (General) 4.5.1975. Reading SR yard closed to goods traffic 2.1970.

Route and traffic: The line leaves the Blackwater Valley at Sandhurst Halt and climbs at a maximum of 1 in 100 to the summit at Crowthorne. It descends more gradually to Winnersh Triangle, then climbs through Earley before another descent to the outskirts of Reading. There is a final climb to Reading (General). The line has always been of value for both passenger and freight movement, generated both locally and between Kent and the Midlands, and further afield. Wokingham is the junction with the LSWR line from Waterloo, thus giving the latter company access to Reading. This section sees a frequent electric train service from Waterloo, the stopping trains from Redhill and Guildford, trains from Gatwick Airport (which began 4.5.1975) and occasional trains from further afield. Until the 1960s there was much heavy freight from both Feltham and along the North Downs line through Guildford. A vast increase in housing and light industry from the 1970s ultimately led to the opening of a new intermediate station just beyond Winnersh.

Reading to Basingstoke (GWR)

Stations in Berkshire: Reading West (¾m from Reading General), Southcote Junction (no station; 1¾m), Mortimer (7½m); other stations in Hampshire.

Opening and closure: Reading to Southcote Junction – see 'Taunton and West of England

line' section below. Southcote Junction to Basingstoke opened 1.11.1848. A goods-only line from Southcote Junction to Coley (1¾m) – referred to as Central Goods – opened 4.5.1908 and closed 25.7.1983. Reading West opened 1.7.1906 at Oxford Road Junction. A spur from Oxford Road Junction to West Junction on the Bristol main line opened 22.12.1856.

Route and traffic: The line heads south from Oxford Road Junction, descending moderately for over 2 miles before climbing almost to Mortimer. After leaving the outskirts of Reading the line passes through land that to this day is little developed. The line is an important link from the South to the North and West and continues to see both freight and passenger trains on a regular basis. Additionally a frequent local passenger service is provided between Reading and Basingstoke. A DMU depot has been built in the vee of Oxford Road Junction.

Main lines west of Reading

Bristol and South Wales line (GWR)

Stations in Berkshire: Reading General (36m from Paddington), Tilehurst (38¾m), Pangbourne (41½m); other stations outside Berkshire.

Opening and closure: The line from Reading to Steventon (just beyond Didcot) opened 1.6.1840. Tilehurst opened 1882.

Route and traffic: Immediately west of Reading were goods yards on the north side and a locomotive depot on the south side. The former is now an engineers' yard and the latter a diesel maintenance depot. Beyond this is West Junction, with a spur to Oxford Road (see 'Reading to Basingstoke' above). The line follows the River Thames in a series of graceful curves, crossing the river at the site of Goring troughs and passing into Oxfordshire. The line is used by expresses to Bristol and South Wales, cross-country trains from the South to the Midlands and beyond, and local services. It is also heavily used by freight trains.

Taunton and West of England line (GWR)

Stations in Berkshire: Reading (36m from Paddington), Reading West (36¾m), Southcote Junction (no station; 37¾m), Theale (41¼m), Aldermaston (44¾m), Midgham (46¾m), Thatcham (49½m), Newbury Racecourse (52½m), Newbury East Junction (no station; 52¾m), Newbury (53m), Enborne Junction (no station; 54¼m), Kintbury (58½m), Hungerford (61½m); other stations outside Berkshire.

Midgham was called Woolhampton until 1873.

Opening and closure: Reading to Hungerford opened 21.12.1847. Reading West opened 1.7.1906 as an interchange station for cross-country services, but is now used solely by local trains. Newbury Racecourse was, as the name implies, used mainly for race traffic. It opened to regular passenger trains 3.10.1988, initially on an experimental basis, and is still open.

Route and traffic: The line curves sharply on a rising gradient immediately after leaving Reading to reach Oxford Road Junction, then Southcote Junction, where is turns west. It follows the Kennet & Avon Canal all the way to the county boundary. After leaving Southcote Junction and the extremities of Reading, the line passes through several industrial areas, interspersed with attractive countryside. Beyond Newbury the scenery improves greatly as the line continues along the Kennet Valley to Hungerford. The line is used by expresses to and from Taunton and the West of England, and local trains, which run as far as Bedwyn. There are still several freight sidings in operation, notably at Theale for oil, stone and cement. There were sidings at Aldermaston for the nearby Atomic Weapons Research Establishment, but these have been closed. Through freight trains mostly convey stone from the Mendips, initially to Acton.

Didcot, Newbury & Southampton line (DNSR)

Newbury to Didcot

Stations in Berkshire (1960s boundaries): Hermitage (4½m from Newbury), Pinewood Halt (5¼m), Hampstead Norris (7½m), Compton (9½m); other stations in Oxfordshire.

Opening and closure: The line opened from Newbury East Junction 13.4.1882. Pinewood Halt opened 11.9.1933. The line closed to passengers 11.9.1962 and to freight 10.8.1964.

Route and traffic: The line climbed out of the Kennet Valley to the Berkshire Downs at a ruling gradient of 1 in 106 to a point just beyond Hermitage, from where it dropped at the same rate to Hampstead Norris. It then climbed again, still with a maximum of 1 in 106 through Compton and into Oxfordshire. The line was built as part of a north-south link, and despite expectations never prospered from its passenger services. The only time it saw heavy traffic was during the Second World War, when demand was such that in 1943 the line was doubled. Even towards the closure of the line, freight was far more active than passenger services.

Newbury to Southampton

Stations in Berkshire: None.

Opening and closure: The line from Enborne Junction to Winchester opened 4.5.1885 and closed to passengers 7.3.1960 and freight 3.2.1964. Enborne Junction was formally out of use from 2.8.1965.

Route and traffic: The line turned south at Enborne Junction, climbing at 1 in 106 through open countryside to the county boundary immediately before Woodhay. Traffic as 'Newbury to Didcot' section above.

Lambourn branch (GWR)

Stations in Berkshire (1960s boundaries): Newbury West Fields Halt (¾m from Newbury), Speen (1¾m), Stockcross & Bagnor (2¾m), Boxford (4¾m), Welford Park (6¼m), Great Shefford (8¼m), East Garston (10m), Eastbury Halt (11m), Lambourn (12½m). Speen was called Speen for Donnington until 1932. Great Shefford was West Shefford until 11.1902.

Opening and closure: The line opened 2.4.1898 and closed 4.1.1960, except for the section from Newbury to Welford Park, which was retained for MOD use until 7.8.1972. A branch to an American Airforce Base from Welford Park (3m) opened 1954. The line closed to all traffic 3.11.1973. Newbury West Fields Halt opened 1.10.1906 and closed 4.2.1957.

Route and traffic: For the first half-mile the branch ran parallel to the main line on a rising gradient. It then crossed the Kennet & Avon Canal and headed north along the Lambourn Valley, climbing at a maximum of 1 in 60, followed by a short fall at a similar gradient at Stockcross. It climbed again to Welford Park, then was level to Great Shefford, followed by another climb at a maximum of 1 in 60 almost to Eastbury Halt. It continued to be undulating, with a final climb into the terminus. In addition to passengers and general goods traffic, there was movement of horses to and from Lambourn. As well as steam-hauled trains, GWR diesel railcars were very often used. The Airforce Base near Welford Park generated considerable traffic.

G. W. R.

READING

INDEX OF LOCATIONS